Christian Logic 2

THE BIBLE AND SCIENCE

Dr. Thomas Childs

Book Layout ©2017 BookDesignTemplates.com

Ordering Information:

Quantity sales. Special discounts are available on quantity purchases by corporations, associations, and others. For details, contact the "Special Sales Department" at the address above.

ISBN 978-1505412413

Contents

Introduction: Christian Logic 2 79

1 Finding Common Ground 4

2 God and The Big Bang 20

3 The Bible and Evolution..43

4 Science and The Future 56

5 God and The Big Bang...68

Author: Dr. Thomas Childs 77

I dedicate this book to my dad and mom.

Dad -who has given me a great appreciation for science and philosophy, from taking me stargazing in the backyard as a boy, to always encouraging me to think carefully and critically.

Mom-who has passed on to me her deep and abiding faith, no matter the storms or challenges in life.

*The stars in the heavens and the cosmos itself
lead us to God, not away from Him.
Psalm 19*

Dr. Thomas Childs

Christian Logic 2

I once had a very memorable lunch conversation with a good friend who had asked to meet to discuss a question he had about the Bible. The reason I won't forget it is because he surprised me. Surprised me not in terms of what he said, but more in terms of what he had not said after years of friendship. That being, after years of being friends, after years of allowing me to be his pastor, and after years of assuming he had a deep understanding of basic Christian doctrine, he surprised me with a statement. "Pastor Thomas, I really appreciate your friendship and your teaching. I very much love Jesus Christ. And I want to believe in the Bible. But honestly, I just can't reconcile believing in the Bible, because I also very much believe in dinosaurs. What am I supposed to do?"

For most Christians, we all have at least some type of similar questions raised by problems between what we have learned from science and what we know of the Bible. Dinosaurs, the Big Bang, Evolution, Aliens, Miracles, the list is almost endless. And for most, we assume at the onset that we must choose one or the other, science or religion, the Bible or science. But rarely are we adequately informed with a means to incorporate and appreciate both fields of truth. Yes, I use that language intentionally. It is both fields of truth. Yes, Christians and scientists alike ought to be able to embrace both. But it is hard.

Why is appreciating science and religion, especially the Christian Bible and science, so difficult? Bottom line, it simply is not the normal way most of us have been taught. For most, the story is a familiar one. You learn about God and the Bible in church. Science? Well, you learn about that in school and the university. But, learning about religion and science in the same breath? Good luck. You can talk about one or the other, but certainly not both. If you do, you usually are asking for a fight.

It ought to be said up front, I am not really talking about science and religion in this book. There are a myriad of resources, much better than this one, that identify the foundational pieces of both science and religion (in general) and how a person might begin to appreciate and integrate both fields. If you want a personal recommendation, I would encourage you to read Alister McGrath's book, Science and Religion: A New Introduction. The purpose of my writing is intentionally more basic than that, and for a reason. My goal is to offer more of a primer to Christian thinkers who are ready to at least engage the initial questions related to this field of science and Christian logic. It is a field ripe for exploration, and, for me at least, it is amazingly liberating to discover that scientists and Christians can be great friends and partners in discovering God's deeper truths about the world both within and around us.

The point here needs to be clear: Science and Christianity need not be enemies. In fact, it is incredibly liberating to discover how much they support, play off, and even need each other. God gave us the desire to discover and the brains to understand a wealth of information about the world around, within, and beyond us. Neither science nor religion should pull us away from God, rather both should draw us to Him and to a more profound understanding of our place in the cosmos. Even the Bible is clear that the world, the heavens, the earth, the stars, the mountains and the valleys- all of it- should lead us to a deeper understanding and appreciation of both the creation and God (Romans 1:20). Science is a gift from God. So is the Bible and Christianity. It is my firm belief that Christians need to learn to appreciate both. We can, but often it requires a bit more than simple common sense. Often, appreciating both requires a nudge in the right direction. Hopefully this book will do that very thing for you.

CHAPTER 1

Finding Common Ground

Science or Religion? Faith or facts?
Thinking or believing?

W hy is it that so many people through the ages have wrestled with reconciling these two bastions of "truth" known as science and religion? And, how is it that two seemingly fundamental aspects of human existence have found themselves at such odds with one another? From Creation to Evolution, to dinosaurs to Adam and Eve, can a logical, thinking person believe in both? Is that even possible, or must we choose sides?

From the classroom to the church, the university to the family dinner table, few if any other forces have had more of an impact in shaping our lives than science and religion, specifically Western science and Christianity. But, the pressure to choose one or the other has left a scar across the hearts and minds of many sincere, logical people who simply want reasonable answers to questions relating to both fields. Yet, in far too many circles, simple answers are difficult, if not impossible, to come by. This leaves many people wounded and disappointed, being skeptical of either science, religion, or both. Yet, my thesis is that the two are not mutually exclusive. In fact, if taken from the right perspective, science and religion are actually mutually beneficial. Not only do they need each other, but we need them both. And thus, the purpose of this book. My goal is to help us work through the biggest challenges that face bridging the gaps between science and religion (Christianity), in hopes of integrating the most fundamental truths from both fields into everyday life.

The Search for Truth

So, why all the problems? Why all the conflict to begin with? Why can't everyone just get along? You would think that, given the stakes, both science and religion would have been working together from the beginning to find common ground. Yet, this just is not the case. Part of the reason can be attributed to three fundamental issues: First, many people assume that science cannot co- exist with religion; Second, many people in religion assume that God does not reveal "truth" through science; and, Third, the "experts" in both fields tend to cross boundaries, thereby blurring the lines between truth in either field. Of course, there are a myriad of other reasons, but these three present formidable problems for logical, thinking people who want to believe in God and the truths of science. Yet, without working through the issues presented by both, none of us will find balance, health, and personal peace regarding these two fields of learning. So where to start?Hypothesis Versus Fact Versus "Truth"

Let's begin by going back to our classes in high school or college concerning science. Consider the stance our educational systems typically have taken to "avoid" religious statements. It is not "appropriate" to discuss God and creation. It is "out of bounds" to discuss "theories" of how God and evolution may co-exist. We aren't supposed to even talk about issues of moral authority, Intelligent Design, or First Cause. But have you ever wondered why? One reason is, in theory, our schools are to teach indisputable truth! We teach facts! We teach what can be seen, observed, and proved by scientific method. Or, so we say. Why? Because in reality, we are teaching far more scientific theories than anyone likes to admit. Even more, rather than only teaching the cosmos as we know it to be, we also very much are teaching the world as we hypothesize it to be. Why? It is because scientists themselves are coming up with new theories and new hypotheses all the time. It's the nature of their business, it's the nature of their craft.

But therein lies the problem: Define for me exactly the nature of a theory or hypothesis. Is it not some type of unknown, but assumed proposition that is tested with facts that are known or may be determined? Is a theory or a hypothesis not more of an educated guess as to how things work? Is it not more of a proposed, reasonable explanation of something that is not yet explainable? If so, then note: a hypothesis is an idea that has not yet been proven as true, but until that time, it is accepted. Not yet proven to be true, yet accepted anyway. Hmm. Is this so different than many religious claims? Like the existence of God? We have facts that are known (energy exists, but where did the energy in the universe come from? humans have morals, but where did human morality come from? matter exists, but where did all the ingredients of the universe come from?), but those facts lead to both questions, theories, and hypotheses. How ironic that in "truth," science and religion are in fact quite similar in these areas. Both have a myriad of ideas that are accepted based on observable reality, and yet, both have a myriad of ideas that have not yet been physically proven to be true, yet are accepted anyway.

Darkness to Enlightenment and Reason

Imagine the chaos after the demise of the Roman Empire. Western civilization had fallen apart. Barbarians ruled throughout the lands. Most people were uneducated. And, superstitious beliefs were the norm for answering the most difficult questions humanity was facing. The medieval culture relied on perceived magic, mysticism, astrology, and even prayer (although more like "magic wand" prayer) to explain and manipulate the world. As a result, many people attributed illness and misfortune to the presence of demons, witchcraft, the supernatural, etc. How ironic that early scientists were often considered practitioners of witchcraft. The reason is because many attempts at early science appeared to be "magical" (unexplainable) and as such, they were often equated with demons and evil spirits. But wouldn't we expect that? After all, it was the Dark Ages! Of course that's what people would think. The world was flat and there were sea monsters at the end of the earth. Everything that was unexplainable wound up being related to some spiritual something, good or bad.

Science continued its uneasy union with spirituality until the Age of Enlightenment with reformists like John Locke, a philosopher and medical researcher of the 17th and 18th century. He argued for separation of church and state, primarily because he knew that attempts at science should not be linked to spiritual anything. And even today, regardless of your religious or anti-religious views, most of us would say Locke was correct. From that point, the movement grew and grew, to the point that empirical evidence was required as the basis for all rational thought. In hindsight, it is easy to see why such a movement took place. Not only did scientists not want to be identified as witches or warlocks, they also now knew that the popularized magic (yes, some of that even in the church) of the Dark Ages was a sham.

The rapid advances of science continued to reinforce the idea that humanity would eventually find all answers to life's questions though quantifiable research. The new worldview defined the reality of existence by the physical surroundings rather than spiritual aspects of life. As religion and science definitively separated, people were no longer prisoners of superstitions from the Dark Ages, and the pendulum swung to the opposite end of the spectrum. Now, no longer was there such a thing as magic; in fact, mankind was convinced that we no longer needed to believe in anything but observable reality. In just a few hundred years, we had moved from a purely spiritual view in addressing the unexplainable of life, to a worldview that believed observable, explainable science would answer all our questions. In other words, the pursuit of scientific knowledge became the entire framework for humanity's understanding of reality and truth. We still see this attitude through much of the scientific community, if not Western world, today.

Here's the problem putting science on such a pedestal though: tell me, has science answered the most difficult questions facing humanity today? Has the human race actually become better because of all the scientific advancements of the last 500 years? Are we better people? Are we better to each other? Are we even better to ourselves?And thus the rub with all the promise of the Enlightenment and the human idolization of science. Science has not fulfilled its promise to answer our deepest questions, address our darkest issues, and solve our most fundamental human problems. In fact, with the advent of the nuclear bomb, science has potentially just made it all worse, by threatening to destroy all life as we know it. If we do obliterate ourselves with nuclear weapons in WWIII, you tell me, would our world have been better off or worse if scientists, the Enlightenment, and scientific method had never come along?

Is it that science is evil? No. But what I want us to admit is this: Just look around! Observe. Pay attention and notice how our world has become terribly disillusioned minus a spiritual perspective. And also notice how dangerous our world has become because of all the scientific, technological advancements since the Age of Reason.

From guns and bombs, to aircraft carriers, tanks, sidewinder missiles, and nuclear warheads, it is a far, far more dangerous world today that it was in the Dark Ages. And then this: are we happier? Are we more loving, gracious, forgiving? Are we more at peace? Of course not. One might even argue that, as progressive and advanced as we have become, we are one of the most anxious, angry generations to walk the planet.

In our country alone, just interview anyone who went through the Great Depression and ask them if life was more hectic, unhappy and anxious then, or now. Ask any of that generation if people were more aimless and purpose-less then, or now. More and more, as I talk to people today, the great cry is one of depression, anger, and futility, which I believe was far less prevalent even in the Great Depression. And my belief is that part of the problem is our modern disassociation with any grounding of truth whatsoever. As such, multiple generations today have no point of center, no foundation. As postmodernists, we rarely even have a frame of reference for truth and purpose, much less anything better than that. But just maybe there is better way for all of us.

Blurry Lines

If we consider the purpose of science and religion, it is actually quite surprising to find that they have very similar interests. Believe it or not, both science and religion are in fact similar disciplines that work toward the common goal of "good" for all mankind. Both seek to better the standards by which humanity lives. Both seek to reveal the deeper truths which drive existence itself. Yes, they both have taken different paths to answer questions of absolute truth. But, their common goal of discovering and revealing truth are without question. As to science, science approaches the goal by trying to explain reality in terms of how things work. Religion explains the truth of reality in terms of meaning and purpose behind those things (the why and the who). But, either way, what is the nature of truth in the first place? If something is true, isn't it always absolutely true? The answer is "Yes." To this, both science and religion agree. But the problem is that, far too often, in our pursuit of truth, as humans naturally do, experts from the fields of both science and religion tend to keep talking when they are far removed from their area of expertise. Over and over again we see "blurring of the lines" happening through history such that today, in so many cases, engaging both science and religion tends to just be a confusing mess.

Just a few examples. You may have heard of Richard Dawkins. Dawkins is a world-renown zoologist from Oxford, and he has been heavy in the press lately for writing quite a few books on the non-existence of God, such as The God Delusion. Answer me this: why is a zoologist talking about God at all? Is the existence of God (or not) something we should expect a scientist to spend his time discussing? And, regardless if you agree or disagree with Dawkins, shouldn't someone be raising a red flag as to why Dawkins, a zoologist, is so concerned about writing books on the non-existence of God? Does this really sound like a scientist? Or, is this more akin to Dawkins obviously having a personal agenda, if not a vendetta, against God. He is using his scientific credibility to bolster his anti-religious agenda. And it is not just Dawkins, other scientists across the globe are doing similar things. The point here is to simply say, many people in the scientific if not even world community simply assume that science is the definitive and only source of truth, even religious truth. But if Dawkins and others like him are making "truth statements" about God and religion, have they not crossed the line? Blurry, blurry lines.

But religion has done this too. There is a billboard campaign across our country that offers certain quotes that are "from God." Some say, "Don't make me come down there, God." Or, "I miss how you used to talk to me when you were a kid, God." Or, "What part of 'Thou Shalt not' didn't you understand, God." Some of them are catchy. But you know, some, well, not so much. Like this one, "Big Bang Theory, You've Got To Be Kidding, God." Do you see the problem? The problem is this religious person is doing the reverse of what Dawkins is doing, this time from the church. No more has this been exemplified than in the church's handling of the Galileo incident.

Galileo was born in 1564 and he died in 1642. He is considered one of the greatest scientists to ever live, and his achievements include: building the first astronomical telescope, originating the ideas behind Newton's laws of motion, and confirming the Copernican theory of the solar system. The last reference is particularly relevant because the Copernican theory of the solar system states, in a nutshell, that the earth revolves around the sun. While that may seem like "no big deal" today, in the 1500 and 1600s, everyone believed that the sun revolved around the earth and the earth was the center of the universe. The church believed it; atheists believed it; scientists believed it; the entire world believed this "truth."

In 1530, Copernicus published a book where he basically challenged the idea that the earth was the center of the universe. However, Copernicus died shortly thereafter which brings us to Galileo. When Galileo came along, he picked up the work of Copernicus. And, after years of research, Galileo declared that Copernicus was right and that the earth revolved around the sun. Now honestly, does that sound like a big deal? Of course not. Yet, along came "the church" and they literally condemned Galileo for heresy. One reason is because Galileo's "theories/hypothesis" (yes, the church has hypotheses too) were diminishing the role of human beings in the created order. The thinking was, since God created humans in His image, and since God gave the earth to humans to rule, then obviously, humans (and thus the earth we inhabit) are the center of the universe. By saying that the earth was not the center of the universe, Galileo was in essence saying that the Bible was wrong.

At the time, church leaders held a great deal of power, and religious heresy was a criminal offense punishable by death. Since Galileo would not initially recant his theories, the church tried him by Inquisition, and under the threat of prison and torture, they forced Galileo to renounce his belief that the earth revolved around the sun. Ever since that time, many antagonists to the church have pointed to this Galileo incident as proof that the church is full of ignorant people who reject the obvious truths of science in favor of superstition and weak-minded religion. But here is my question. Back to Dawkins, was the church in essence not doing the same thing that the great scientist, Dawkins, is doing in his book, *The God Delusion?*

Here's the way I see it. No matter your side of the fence, plenty of reasons exist for an emotionally charged feud. There is plenty of both reason and suspicion concerning motive and method for science and religion alike. Of course, whatever side of the fence you are on, you can't be the antagonist. Instead, it's always those other people. In this line of thinking, people on both sides adopt righteous indignation over their conviction that "those other people" are intentionally confusing the masses and leading them away from "the truth." After all, science is about truth. Or, religion is about truth. But certainly, not both. It is the university, the school systems, the world scientific community, or churches, preachers and religious leaders all conspiring against everyone else, or as Seinfeld says 'yada, yada, yada'.

The point is to say that when it comes to making authoritative statements, scientists need to stick to the field of science, while the church needs to stick to spiritual matters. Whenever either side crosses those boundaries, they both lose credibility because now both sides of "truth" are being undermined. And lest we doubt this phenomenon, I point again to the rise of Postmodernism, an entire generation of young adults who reject both science and religion, to instead believe that all truth is relative. This is not a good sign for our future. Truth matters. Truth is not relative. And the more science and religion fight with each other, the less both sides will be taken seriously by our children, younger generations, and the outside world. We need common ground. Science and religion need to be friends!!!

Common Ground

Albert Einstein has a great quote from his 1954 essay, "Science and Religion," where he says, "Science without religion is lame, religion without science is blind." One can interpret this on multiple levels. First, it is simply the idea that the greatest scientific advancements (such as atomic energy), if placed in the hands of unethical people, can wind up being totally devastating. Or, the greatest people of faith can be ignorant fools if they persecute a scientist for saying the earth is the center of the universe. But past this, there is the underlying idea that science actually has a basis in faith just like religion, while religion utilizes many aspects of science in every walk of life. In truth, not only do science and religion need each other, but they actually have far more similarities than differences.

On the one hand, although science may claim to deal strictly with ideas that are derived from observation, experimentation, and repetition, in truth, even such a process demands faith at some point too. For example, scientists have faith that there is a Law of Physics behind the universe that gives credence to their scientific theories. Even more, how can anyone trust those laws of Physics, except by faith? How do you know the chair will support you when you sit on it, or the light switch will turn the light on, or the cell phone will dial your parents every time you use the same number?

If we had no faith in the laws of physics, then no one would ever drive, turn on a light, or use a cell phone. When you turn a switch back to the "on" position, you have faith that it will work and you have the science making it work. But it is only the faith in the science that causes you to go back to the light switch over and over again, just as it is only their faith in the laws of physics that causes the scientists to believe in their science at all. We all have faith, it is simply what we place our faith in that matters. The point of religion is to say, we need to have faith in the right things, things that bring meaning and significance not only today, but for all eternity.

On the other hand, religion without science (including a methodology of observation, experimentation, and repetition) is impossibly myopic and short-sighted. Sadly, stubborn adherence to "blind faith" has often provided an easy excuse for intellectual laziness on the part of religious supporters. It is not OK to say something makes no sense, but then "just believe it anyway." It is not OK to say, it makes no sense to believe whatever, but you should just have faith and believe it anyway. Over and over and over again we are reminded that God is the one who gave us brains, and God expects us to use them. Faith should never be used as a replacement for thinking, for when that happens, bad things are bound to ensue. Lest you doubt that, look no further than Hitler and the millions of people who blindly followed him. God gave us the ability to reason with that three and a half pounds of gray matter we call brains, and that, in and of itself, indicates that God expects people to use those brains to their fullest extent. As such, we all, both science and religion, must give ourselves permission, if not responsibility, to explore questions raised by both fields until we have answers that satisfy even the most passionate seeker. It is a journey to become informed in our faith and science, so that we can answer all three questions of how, why, and who, which literally builds a foundation for balanced, holistic living.

Which leaves us where? Well, it ought to leave us wanting to learn from both, while also doing whatever possible to avoid the idea of having "blind faith" in either discipline. Seriously though, why not learn from both? Why not build an informed truth by seeking to understand the best of both religious and scientific claims? Why not keep your brain with you, rather than check it out at the door when you enter a church or a university classroom? Science and religion are not mutually exclusive. You do not have to choose sides. You can believe in both. The point of this book is to say that indeed, science and religion are friends, but often it will only happen in new, open-minded ways of thinking that go contrary to what many are teaching in our society. Rather than raising barriers between the two perspectives, we need to find common ground. We need to seek common understanding. We need to appreciate both.One more step

If you want to know where science and religion meet, start by considering the way that the "experience" of music picks up where the mechanism that makes the music leaves off. Consider a piano, any instrument, an IPOD, or even how your average sound system works. Each of these items has many different components that have the capability to make music. One may have transistors, microphones, amplifiers, and speakers, and each is made of smaller electrical elements like circuits, resistors, and capacitors that have been discovered and built through scientific research. When we connect them all together, these components relay electric and magnetic currents and frequencies that produce sound. There is science behind the electronic components. The science explains how the sound system works to create the music. Science concentrates on the mechanism. Science explains the "how."

The "religion" of music is found in the experience of the music itself. It is the "why' you have the sound system to begin with. The religion is to experience the music, to listen to music and to enjoy music. The mechanism of the sound system is marvelous in its own right, but without the music itself, what purpose does the sound system serve? It would be silent; and as such, it would be useless. Sound systems without sound are without purpose or meaning. Human life without joy, hope, peace, and a true (eternal) future is also without meaning. Thus, as science gives us the mechanism of life, so does religion offer the significance and purpose. For the full experience, one must employ both.

In the same way, for the purposes of this book, we will attempt to find the places where science and religion, particularly Christianity, can meet, giving both meaning and function to many of the various issues that sometimes cause controversy between the two disciplines. It will be akin to the idea that, if you take away God and soul, then everything we know, our entire existence is nothing more than a cosmic, scientific accident. On the other hand, if we bring God into the equation, then, not only can we enjoy the unveiling of new and astonishing scientific discoveries, but we can allow those discoveries to move us ever more deeply into our underlying purpose, meaning, and significance in and with all that is around us.

Questions for Reflection:

1. How does science offer us (humanity) truth?

2. How does religion offer us (humanity) truth?

3. Do you feel conflicts exist between science and religion? If so, why?

4. Where does religion blur the lines of science?

5. Where does science blur the lines of religion?

6. What is the basic purpose of science?

7. What is the basic purpose of religion?

8. How might "music" offer one explanation as to where science and religion can meet?

NOTES

CHAPTER 2

God and The Big Bang

Forced Choices

Imagine a family campfire scene at night- gazing at the stars, crackling fire, hotdogs, smores, smoke rising to the heavens. How many times has this scene repeated itself over the course of human history? The clothes and tents might have been a little different thousands of years ago, but sitting around the campfire is as old a tradition as humanity itself. And not just the campfire, but also the stories told around the campfire. We tell stories of family and friends, adventures and discoveries, real and imagined. And yes, for the longest time, we also have told stories of God. And not just who God is or what God is like, but even more, especially before the advent of science, how God created the heavens and the earth. For millennia, the family campfire gathering was the time for teaching the young, reliving the family's shared heritage, and having conversations about purpose, existence, and yes, also God. As the stars and the campfire lit the night sky, so also did the family elders talk about where those stars came from and how they believed it was all created, and even more, why it was all created. To miss this point about the early campfire stories and teaching God to younger generations is to miss a primary point of the early chapters of Genesis in the Bible.

One reason we do miss this point however is because, today, story-time traditions like the ones around the campfire are the exception rather than the rule. It is a rare experience indeed that families even sit at the dinner table together, much less sit around a campfire and actually talk about the purpose and significance of life. I'm not sure this is a good thing either. How much are our children missing, when they have such rare opportunities to listen to the stories of their elders? How much are younger generations missing by so rarely even talking about God or issues of meaning and purpose in the universe with those who have answers to their questions?

As we have moved into an age that places more value on football and soccer practice than family dinner time, we are increasingly relegating our more important stories to those who care about our children the least. Stories of God, wisdom from elders, conversations of purpose and meaning that previously have been at the center of the family unit have now been replaced by sports and music practice, television and video games. It has not always been this way, and perhaps it should not even be this way now.

That being said, the stories of life, our stories of life, are in essence what the earliest Bible stories in Genesis are all about. It is important not to get hung up on the details. It is important to remember the campfire setting. It is important to not feel like you are forced to choose between the early Bible stories and modern scientific theories. Yes, the two might coincide, but even if they do, that's not the point. Rather, the point is and was to pass along to future generations the most important life answers, such as "Why are we here?" "Where did we come from?" "What is the purpose of life?" These are questions science cannot answer, but they are questions that science can certainly contribute to, if we take the right approach. And everyone needs these answers if ever we are to find true meaning and significance in life.Where Did It All Start?

To begin, I am operating on the assumption that we all understand the basics of The Big Bang Theory and the early Creation account of Genesis 1- 2. Quotes and citations will not be given, neither will I go into the details of those concepts here (if you have not studied both in awhile, it may be helpful to do a quick refresher via internet and Bible reading before you move on). Given that assumption though, the next step is to ask, what do we really know about the beginning of our universe? What are our sources for this understanding? There are as many answers to those questions as stars in the sky. For Christians, often they turn to the creation account in Genesis. For Christians and scientists alike, we also turn to the Big Bang Theory. Beyond this, you can add research, observation, and theory from many prominent scientists who have constructed models to explain the birth of galaxies, the changing nature of the universe as it expands, and particularly relevant to our discussion, its age and origin.

Concerning this Creation event, no one can doubt the current product, the awesome nature of the universe around us. In fact, it is from the "product" in its current state that we derive all of our theories about previous existence. But the problem is, the cosmos as it stands today is so huge that even the brightest of minds must use numbers that defy all logic and comprehension. After all, what does it mean when some scientists say that it takes light about eight minutes to go from the sun to the earth to cover a distance of about 93 million miles? 93 million miles in 8 minutes? Are we supposed to actually comprehend that number?

To put that in perspective, the distance around the entire earth is only 25,000 miles. Only 25,000 miles. Andromeda, the nearest galaxy to us, is about 2.3 million light years away. So, 8 minutes for 93 million miles, and Andromeda is 2.3 million light years away. Seriously? Add to that, any simple internet search will tell you that the best scientists can hardly fathom the actual amount of galaxies in the universe - something to the order of 100 to 200 billion strong. This means there are as many galaxies, galaxies mind you, in the cosmos as there are grains of sand on all the beaches of planet earth. It is simply mind-numbing.

Given the sheer magnitude of the universe, it begs the question, how did it all come to exist? It's one thing if we are talking a little flower or grain of sand (and even that warrants the same question), but it is another thing entirely when you are talking a universe so vast and expansive that our human minds literally do not even have the capacity to grasp its scope. Scientists want to know, and Christians want to know, and Christians who are scientists want to know, "where did it all come from?"

The Big Bang

We begin with science. The Big Bang. We choose the Big Bang because it is the most widely accepted scientific theory of creation, and a host of information on this theory exists as public domain today. Everyone has heard it. We all have been exposed to it. The theory goes something like this. Between 12 and 14 billion years ago, the universe as we know it today was but a speck in the time-space continuum. The heat and pressure from this very dense matter was so great, that it exploded. The resulting explosion was responsible for the continued expansion of everything that exists in the universe today. The outward thrust of matter eventually formed into all of the galaxies, solar systems, stars and elements of the cosmos including our own planet Earth.

How did scientists come to this conclusion? After Einstein introduced the theory of General Relativity, he and many other scientists tried to apply this new concept of gravity as a displacement of space and time to the entire universe. Taking this view required an assumption that matter in the universe was relatively uniform, which basically means you could take one principle from "over here" and apply it to something "over there." One such "something" scientists have used to theorize about the universe is radiation, specifically microwave background radiation. Not to get too technical, the idea is that microwave background radiation basically gives us a snapshot of the oldest light in the universe. Why this matters is because the distribution of this radiation (remnant heat from the Big Bang) appears to have amazing uniformity across the entire sky. So what, perhaps you are asking?

Well, continued research in this area gives modern scientists more and more data that confirms many of their theories as to the beginnings of the cosmos. And by continued research, I am referring to a vast swath of research including pictures from the Hubble space telescope, data collected from radar arrays on Earth, models from the latest computer technology, and on and on. Not only have modern scientists locked in on something profound, in truth, with each new discovery (ie, as Hubble improves, helium gas discoveries, fusion discoveries, Red Shift theories, etc), the Big Bang theory seems increasingly incontrovertible.

Given all of that, of course it makes some sense that most scientists would trace the origins of the universe back to a single point in time. And in all honesty, if their evidence is that compelling, why wouldn't Christians do the same? Why not listen to what the universe is teaching us? Why not open our minds to whatever it is our greatest scientists have to say? Which brings us to the issue of the initial "bang."

Scientists Who Avoid a Creator

The primary problem for most of us is not what happened after the Big Bang. We will get into various Christian interpretations of how we can reconcile the early chapters of Genesis with the Big

Bang theory. No, the problem in point of fact is where that first speck of matter came from to begin with? And not only that, but where did the energy for that initial explosion come from? Who organized that initial speck such that it would explode into an unimaginably vast and complex cosmos? Yes, we can agree with scientists that the evidence we have today points to an initial explosion that set in motion the universe. And yes, we can agree that this explosion happened at a certain point in time about 13-14 billion years ago. But, what about the point in time immediately before the Big Bang?

Some scientists who want to avoid the possibility of bringing "God" into the conversation will simply say, nothing existed before the Big Bang. And after that, the "speck" simply appeared out of nothing, and then BANG! Our universe with 100 billion galaxies was created by and from nothing. The "matter" for it all came from nothing. The energy required for the explosion came from nothing. The structure, organization, and design of it all came from nothing. The bottom line being, "Nothing Created Everything."

Nothing created everything. Everything came from nothing. Talk about a lack of logic. Is that even remotely logical? Does it make any amount of sense to say, "Nothing created everything?" And yet, for scientists who want to avoid a Creator, their answer is "Absolutely. Yes. Nothing created everything." But for those of us who are willing to entertain the idea of a Creator, that simply makes no sense. And, there are at least four issues that are particularly problematic for supporters of a "Nothing created everything" approach. These issues surface when we tackle the questions of Origin, Purpose, Design, and Intelligibility. Taken separately, each one outlines a major challenge for the premise that "Nothing created everything." Collectively, the arguments point out serious flaws with any theory that excludes the possibility of a Creator.Question of Origins

We can begin with a question of origins. Even before we had scientific evidence of a Big Bang, the basis for a theological case supporting a Creator was developed between the 11th and 12th centuries. It was known as the Kalam Cosmological Argument.

Basic points of this argument are:

(1) Everything that has a beginning of its existence has a cause of its existence.

(2) The universe has a beginning of its existence.

Therefore:

(3) The universe has a cause of its existence.

(4) If the universe has a cause of its existence then that cause is God. Therefore:

(5) God exists.

(For these points and more, see *The Kalam Cosmological Argument*, by William Lane Craig, Wipf & Stock pub, 2000)

The focal point here being: whatever has a beginning also must have a cause. And yes, some will argue that the universe has no beginning. But if you do, then you essentially reject the Big Bang theory. I don't reject the Big Bang theory, so we won't pursue the infinite universe theories here. What I do want to pursue is what we all know with common sense: if something has a beginning, it also must have a cause. This is simple logic. And countless incredibly brilliant thinkers over the years agree, including Bonaventure in the 13th century, John Locke, in the 17th century, David Hume and Immanuel Kant in the 18th century, things with a beginning must have a cause.

To put this in everyday language, we can think of this in terms of negative data. Negative data meaning what is not there, what is not going to happen in everyday life, reveals a truth about reality. For example, if you like to grill, who believes that, if we walk to your back porch, open your grill and wait long enough, eventually steak, chicken, or sausage will appear there? Or, whoever gets worried that one day, while driving down the highway, the Pacific

Ocean will appear on the interstate? Do you ever fret over the possibility that an Egyptian pyramid will mysteriously appear in your hallway and block the path to your bathroom? Of course not. But why not? It's because of our absolute belief in the principles of causality and being.

You will never worry about things suddenly appearing out of thin air, because you know with absolutely certainty that such things never happen. When you drive down the interstate, you focus on the drivers around you, the road, warning signs, and the kids who are playing the "no touching" game in the back seat, but you never worry about an ocean liner suddenly popping into existence at the stop light. This is what Kalam was talking about, and there is no question that this is how we believe the world works today.

So why would we think the beginning of the universe was any different? And the obvious, most logical answer is, it wasn't. Regarding the questions of origins, everything that has a beginning has a cause. The universe had a beginning (it did not appear out of thin air), therefore the universe had a cause. That cause is God, therefore, God, the First Cause, exists.

The Question of Purpose

Let's move on to the next item, the question of purpose. The point here is not to answer the question of purpose (that is in my last book, Christian Logic), rather it is to glance at the question, What can science tell us about the reason humans exist in this world? What can scientists tell us about "Why everything is here in the first place?" And we know the answer. Science simply has no response, much less an answer as to the "why" of existence. It isn't their fault, rather science is simply ill equipped to answer the question "Why was it all created?" Or, "Why are we here?" Granted, scientists can tell us many things about how it all works, but when it comes right down to it, explaining the purpose of it all is not in their domain. Why that matters for our discussion is that the question of purpose itself points to the idea of a Creator. Without a Creator, the creation has no purpose. But with a Creator, the equation shifts entirely.

Question of Design

Concerning the question of design, the basic issue relates to how impossible it would be for such a complex system as the universe to somehow design itself from nothing. And not only all the intricacies of the cosmos, but even the laws that govern the cosmos. For example, gravity must be sufficient to hold atmosphere and to stabilize the orbit of the moon, but not so much that it crushes everything above 3 feet tall. Or heat and cold. Most of us have heard at some point that if our earth was even a few feet closer or father away from the sun, huge changes in our climate would change life as we know it, if not eradicate all life entirely. Or the presence of the moon. How might our earth be different if the moon didn't affect the tides? Or water. Where else in the cosmos have we even found water, much less so much of it as exists on our earth. Without water, where would we be? And not just water, what about rain? Or photosynthesis? Or? The list is beyond endless. There are so many singularities for our planet alone to sustain life that the odds of having life at all without intelligent design putting it all together is absolutely implausible.

Question of Intelligibility

And then there is the issue of intelligibility itself. Einstein said it best. Something to the effect of, the most difficult thing to understand about the cosmos, is that we are sitting here, reading this book, trying to understand our own questions about the cosmos. It's like, the very idea that we are even arguing about how the universe was created suggests something beyond the universe which created us. More than that, human beings exist as thinking, curious people on a relentless quest to understand the world and universe around us. The natural question is "why do we even care?" Lions don't. Monkeys don't care. Raccoons, elephants, dogs, cats, worms, mice, none of them ever ask the question why? But we do. Talk about an argument for being created in the image of God. What else explains our questions? Furthermore, the passion that surrounds our quest to know and understand is well beyond simple curiosity. It is part of our essence. So why is humanity different? What causes the questioning and the drive and focus for answers and the acquisition of knowledge?

One answer points to the fact that, since we can comprehend our world, it would seem that the Creator wants us to comprehend it. We are created with intelligence, curiosity, and a yearning to understand. We are also created within a planetary system that is perfectly tuned to support not any life, but our lives, such that we are uniquely positioned with "front row seats" to develop that very understanding. God wants us to observe, explore, and research the wonders around us.

The argument of intelligibility is actually encouraging, because it says that God wanted us to think intelligently precisely because God wants our intelligence and quest for knowledge to lead us to Him. In other words, the creation itself, and all the scientists who study it, is in fact the vehicle for us to know God better, not the opposite. Thus, the stars, the mountains, the valleys, the oceans, the sunsets as well as mankind's desire to experience and understand all of them is in and of itself the argument for God's existence. As such, our ability to use science and to desire deeper understandings of the cosmos is not a matter of survival of the fittest or natural selection, rather it is a clear indicator of intelligibility and a First Cause. In essence, the entire equation simply points to one unavoidable conclusion: "I can come to my own conclusions, therefore God exists."

The Bible as a Source of Knowledge

So let's use the former arguments as a springboard into the Bible and science in general. And even more, as Christian Logic, let's also assume, for the sake of argument, that it is critical for Christians to reconcile the early chapters of the Bible with the latest scientific theories of Creation like the Big Bang Theory. Given these goals, it should be stated up front that a myriad of issues exist that should at some point be addressed. Who really wrote the Bible? How was God involved? How does the Bible relate to science? How should we interpret the Bible? What parts of the Bible are relevant to our conversation with science? Which are not? Most of those questions are not for this book. But a few of them at least need a cursory explanation, starting with the issue of science and religion in general. That being, just what is the Bible in the first place and what is it not? The short answer is that the Bible is a theology book. It is not a science book.

Let's explore why the Bible is not a science book. To begin, it is critical to note that the Bible is not and was never intended to be a definitive book of all knowledge. What this means is that, while the Bible offers very relevant, profound, and necessary truths for humanity to understand and personalize, we also know that countless vats of knowledge come to us from every other nook and cranny of the world. The Bible is one authority for truth, yes, but the Bible is not the authority for all truth. God gave us brains, which means our ability to reason and think and experience life is also a way to learn truth.

The incorrect assumption would be that what God gave us in the Bible includes everything He wants us to know or understand about whatever particular subject we find in the biblical text. But when you think this through, it just makes no sense. Could you imagine the size of God's physics textbook that gave every minute detail of how God created the sun or stars? Could you imagine the size of the chemistry book that included all of God's knowledge for the process behind all chemical reactions in the cosmos? In truth, if we chose even one scientific explanation for how a given thing works, including the molecular physics behind that thing, the textbook would be incomprehensible. The Bible is not a science book, and it was never intended to be. This finally brings us to the source of contention for so many scientists and Christians alike, Gen 1-2, the Creation account.

Where Christians often get into trouble is when they attempt to reconcile the latest scientific theories (ie, the Big Bang) with a very cursory reading of Genesis 1-2. Why the trouble? It is because rather than reading Gen 1-2 through the lens of theology, we attempt to read and interpret those chapters through the lens of science. And understand, it can be done, however, it is incredibly important that we all remember that's not the point. The point of the Bible is never to tell us "how" anything scientific works, or "how" God did anything. Again, that's not the point. Does this mean we cannot or should not speculate on such things? Of course not. God gave us brains, let's work it through. However, the point is to say that our primary task with the Bible is to ask "why?" and "who?" and then learn from the scientists as to "how."

The Biblical Text

A summary: The text from Genesis 1 and 2 basically tells us that God created everything in the beginning. Such as, God created the heavens and the earth. At first, the earth was formless and void, darkness was over the surface of the deep, and the Spirit of God was hovering over the waters. And God said, "Let there be light." And there was light. And God saw that the light was good, and he separated the light from the darkness. God called the light day, and he called the dark, night. And there was evening, and there was morning the first day. Then, throughout the rest of Genesis chapter 1, we are told the story of God creating it all in six days, and on the seventh day God rested.

Before the Age of Enlightenment, everyone generally accepted these early teachings of the Bible at face value. After all, why wouldn't they? When it rained, God was crying, when it thundered, God was stomping His feet. When you got sick, you invoked God (or the gods) for healing, and when you had a bountiful harvest, God (or the gods) must be pleased. With such a worldview, no one thought twice about God creating the cosmos in 6, 24 hour days and resting on the 7th day. After all, why would they?

However, after the Enlightenment and Age of Reason, more and more people began to question the "face value" reading of Gen 1-2. And again, why wouldn't they? After all, a cursory reading of these 2 chapters was increasingly coming in conflict with what experience and reason was teaching us. As such, we should question old, Dark Age assumptions, shouldn't we? And we did. Christians and scientists both have struggled with how to reconcile these first few chapters of Genesis with all the discoveries the scientists made and continue to make concerning creation, beginnings, and origins. I would submit though, there has been far too much needless anxiety, conflict, and animosity between both groups. Why? We simply have not been exposed to a variety of reasonable, common domain options.

Interpretations of The Creation Account: Genesis 1-2

So what are our options, if indeed we want to reconcile the prevailing scientific discoveries of creation, like the Big Bang, with the historical doctrines of the faith? And for that, I offer you 5 options that are in public domain today. In truth, these options can become intricate and complicated, to which you may want to refer to more detailed resources such as an Introduction to the Old Testament, or a myriad of books relating specifically to each perspective (start with an internet, Wikipedia search and then go from there). In fact, after studying these options, my hope is that you might pursue in more detail the option that makes sense to you, with goal of perhaps coming up with your own version of God, creation, and science that works for you. Wow. Are we even allowed to "think for ourselves" in this matter? And the answer, of course! That's the point. Realize, no one has the perfect answer on this except God. And if anyone claims such an answer, and you are pretty sure they are not God, perhaps you ought to be concerned. Think for yourself. God gave you a brain. Use it. Learn your options, then come up with your own theory based on evidence, study, facts, your experience, and scripture. As for the rest, enjoy the conversation, but certainly don't let it become a stumbling block to your faith.

Option 1: Religion Excluding Science
7, 24 hour Day Theory

This is the most common interpretation of Gen 1-2, and unfortunately, the most problematic. It is the idea that God created the universe in seven distinct 24-hour periods that align with our watches, clocks, and calendars. Advocates of this theory often refer to the use of the word "day" in Genesis as a literal and specific number of 24 hours. This approach to the Genesis account does not acknowledge any of the scientific discoveries from Hubble, the Big Bang, or whatever else. Consequently, supporters of this theory believe that there were no dinosaurs, there was no Ice Age, and the universe is only about 6000 years old. The theory does not leave room for a Big Bang because the Bible doesn't mention it. As a result, this most common interpretation is the very one that gives both scientists and scientifically inclined Christians absolute fits, because it simply does not match the evidence offered by the world and cosmos around us. I might even add, in so many respects, this interpretation actually rejects the evidence that God gave us. After all, who gave us the ability to learn from the cosmos and world around us, if not God? Who gave us the cosmos and the earth to learn from? God. To be clear, the purpose is not to judge people who believe this interpretation, but it is to say, in "making friends between science and religion," this is not the best approach. And in truth, there are many other options that both accept the authority of the Bible as well as the authority of scientists today. Which brings us to option 2.

Option 2: Sacred Week Theory

This theory says Genesis 1-2 has no intention of describing "How" God created the universe at all. In fact, to even go there is to reject the Bible's intent. In this, the idea of the Hebrew word, "Day," is nothing more than that, an idea. As such, "day" has nothing to do with our understanding of time, clocks, or calendars. Rather, the idea of "day," especially "seven days" is nothing more than a very broad concept used by the ancient Hebrews to define an idea of completion. For example, I could say to my wife, "Wow, this was a really, really good day." At first glance, you might assume I am talking about something good that happened to me at work. But what if I were to say that you completely missed the point? Why? Because today, at 3 am my son was born. My son, who 8 years ago we were told we could not have children. My son, who 3 years ago we had a series of miscarriages. My son, who 9 months ago was conceived amid huge anxieties and fears. My son, who 3 days ago caused false contractions. My son, who 24 hours ago brought us to the hospital. My son, who a few minutes ago was born healthy and whole and is now nestled softly in the arms of his mother and everyone is healthy. This has been a very, very good "day." We are not talking a calendar, rather we are talking about a season of life, a period of time, a "concept' that resulted in a fabulous conclusion.

For the ancient Hebrews, seven days represents the concept of completion. Since the number seven is viewed as a perfect or holy number, the point of seven days in Genesis might be to specifically convey the idea of sacred completion. Thus, the entire time of creation, whether it is 13 billion years or some other calculation based on future scientific discoveries, it is simply a "Sacred Week" or a set apart period of time to God that ended with something very, very good. This time was holy complete with the purpose of creating life on the planet earth because God wanted to be in relationship with that life.

With this view, who cares how long God took to complete the process? Rather, what matters is, God did complete the process, on God's time, and the result was very, very good. What a great "day" it was, on the "7th day," when God rested, and looked over all he had made, and held His new creation in His arms.

Option 3: Age-Day theory

The Age-Day theory focuses very specifically on the Hebrew word for "Day" in this passage of Genesis. The word is "YOM." It is not talking about a day on our calendar. It is the concept that the Lord does not look at time like we do; a day for the Lord is a thousand years. So in the case of Creation, one day represents billions of years. In short, a day in this context refers to a certain age of time in which God did everything the scientists say happened. Perhaps Day one represents 8 billion years. Day 2 represents 4 billion years. Day 3 represents 1 billion years. Day 4 represents 500 million years. Day 5 represents 100 million years. And Day 6 represents 6000 years? No matter the math, the point is simply that the entire Creation event happened over the course of six time periods. During the seventh "day/age," God rested. The accumulated time from all seven of the time periods adds up to the latest scientific theories, such as 13 billion years.

Option 4: Gap Theory

The Gap Theory focuses on "reading between the lines" of Gen 1:1 and Gen 1:2. Genesis 1:1 says that God created the heavens and the earth in the beginning, but only in very general language. Verse

2 and beyond, then, talks about specifics. Gap theory is an attempt to reconcile scientific time estimates with the biblical account by allowing for a "gap" between the first two verses. Advocates for this theory assert that Gen 1 includes an indefinite period of time, perhaps 13 billion years, during which the geological ages took place. During this time, the dinosaurs lived. Around the time of the ice age of 200,000 years ago, a supernatural disaster occurred destroying much of creation and making these animals extinct. Then, beginning in Gen 1:2, the six days of creation described by the Bible actually refer to six periods of time in which God recreated the earth after the Ice Age. Just as an aside, proponents of this theory sometimes use the same approach to explain the timing of events in the book of Revelation. As with Genesis, they suggest that there is a "gap" or a suspension of the recorded Biblical timeline to describe the unpredictable amount of time for the age that will elapse between the ascension of Jesus and the date of his future return to earth. I bring that up because it relates to our next theory.

Option 5: Revelation-Day Theory

The Revelation-Day Theory supports the idea that Creation took place over billions of years as science has determined, but it was revealed to the writer in "word pictures" of several, 24 hour days. They use the imagery used in the book of Revelation as an example to illustrate the principle. Revelation 20:11 says, "Then I saw all the dead standing before the great white throne, and they were judged according to what they had done." The idea is that there probably is not going to be a single file line with billions upon billions of people at the judgment; rather, this is a "word picture" trying to convey a certain truth. In a similar way, Genesis 1-2 gives us word pictures of God Creating the Universe. The truths are there in content, just not in form.

Option 6: Eden-Only Theory

One final option for our conversation (there are many more, and everything in-between) is the Eden-Only theory. Advocates of this theory confine the scriptures about Creation to a limited context, that being the Garden of Eden. The idea here is simply that Gen 1-2 relate only to the Garden of Eden (even though it is a big garden), and thus no conclusions about the rest of God's creation event ought to be drawn from this text.Creation Meets Science

Which leaves us where? To which I ask, what do you think? Surprised I would ask you that question? Well, don't be. The point of all of this is for you to personally figure out which option works the best for you and your scientific and religious approach to God and creation. Do you realize, it is VERY OK for you to choose? Why in the world so many of us feel compelled to accept the answers of other people on this one is beyond me. But this is certain, there are many plausible answers. The key is, understand your options, then work it out for yourself. Don't let this issue of the Big Bang, or Creation in the Bible, or "whatever" be a stumbling block to your faith in God. Rather, allow this study and your own observations of the cosmos to open your mind to the wonder of what God has done. For me, the answer lies in a shared relationship between science and religion. Both have truth to offer, and both can be embraced if only we look at the picture from a slightly different angle.

The point in offering all of this information about the two perspectives is simply to say that science and religion can meet here. It is not an either-or proposition. You can believe in Jesus, the Bible, and the Big Bang. The scientific theories may be proven to be historically accurate or not, but the presence of scientific explanations which are relevant to everyday life should never, ever cause a person to walk away from God. In fact, the message in Romans 1:20 tells us that the questions of the universe, in fact of the very existence of the universe itself, should draw us to God, not away from God. "The creation itself...Since the very beginnings of human beings gazing into the stars from their family campfires.... they have clearly observed God's invisible attributes. Now, we also study and document them, so that all people are without excuse (Rom 1:20ish)."

As our ancestors gathered around the campfire and looked to the stars, we can almost hear the voice of the tribal elder who tells the story of Genesis. God created the Heavens and the Earth, and they are here to remind us just how much He loves us. The storyteller gestures to the endless stars in the night sky and says, "See, God loved you and me and all of our tribe so very much that he made all that you can see just for us to enjoy. He gave it all to us so that we would have something that we could see and touch that would always remind us of just how amazing He is, and how much He loves us, and how much we are His family. He built us a home. Even more, as great as He is, God will do everything to be in a relationship of love with us, because we are His family. All that you can see is God's way of saying 'See how much I, your heavenly Father, love you'."

This is the true common ground between science and religion regarding our beginnings. It is to grasp our own place and significance and meaning in a vast universe that defies comprehension, but allows at least some understanding of its reality and where we fit in. The Bible gives us the foundation of God and His purpose for creating us, His children, and the magnificence of all God's work, our temporary home. Science gives us the details. But as amazing as it all is, both point to the need to see beyond the cosmos itself as a physical possession. The point is the people, you and me, that God created and placed in that creation so that these children, us, might be open to being family with Him and one another. As amazing as it sounds, the cosmos is little more than an environment God made for us, so that we could be in everlasting relationship with Him. Even more, as our modern scientists increasingly discover just how vast and unimaginably great the cosmos is, this should draw us to God, not away from Him, because it displays the amazing nature of this home God has built us. In the past, science added very little to our understandings of how amazing this temporary home truly is. Today, with science by our side, all of it is more logical than ever.

Questions for Reflection:

1. What conflicts potentially exist between the Big Bang theory and a typical interpretation of Genesis 1-2?

2. What are some potential flaws in saying "nothing created everything?"

3. What is the Kalam Cosmological argument? How does it provide a platform for understanding the origins of the cosmos?

4. How does the issue of "design" affect our understandings of beginnings?

5. How does the issue of "intelligibility" affect our understandings of beginnings?

6. Name the 6 theories of creation. Which one is your favorite? Why?

7. Can people disagree as to which theory of creation is "the truth," yet still be Christians? If so, why?

NOTES

CHAPTER 3

The Bible and Evolution

Outside of questions related to the origins of the universe, few issues can wreak more havoc on the "logic" of the Christian believer than those regarding issues of evolution. Most of us have been exposed to two very contrasting, competing stories that have gone unresolved in our minds for most of our lives. There is the story of Genesis 1-3, that God created the cosmos and at some point in that creation process God created Adam and Eve. And then there is the story of evolution, that God had very little, if anything, to do with the creation process, especially human beings, and there was no Adam and Eve. The obvious question is, "are these two approaches incompatible?" Is there a way for science to provide the mechanism and religion to provide the music for this evolutionary conversation? And my answer, of course there is common ground.

But per usual, sometimes we just need a little nudge in the right direction.

Where did humans come from?For many of us, scientist or not, the argument for human origins began to take shape somewhere in the early 1800s. Charles Darwin was on his ship, the H.M.S. Beagle, when he found himself on the Galapagos islands in the Eastern Pacific Ocean. In observing the diversity of life on those islands, in observing the strange and exotic animals such as the marine iguana, Darwin soon began to hypothesize as to what led to such incredible diversity of life and the process by which that very life came into existence. It would not be long before his evolutionary theories on mutation, variation, and natural selection would soon be promoted and taught throughout the world.

Hundreds of years later, as so many of us experienced in our science classes in high school or college, the early theories of Darwin have now been replaced with the "facts" of evolutionary theory. It is ironic, that evolutionary theory is taught as fact. But be that as it is, we learn about primordial soup. We learn about amino acid experiments. We observe the natural progression of an ape becoming a human being. We learn about natural selection. We learn about survival of the fittest. All these facts of science seem bulletproof at face value. All these learnings initially make sense. They make sense, at least, until we go back and reread the early Bible stories of Genesis, Adam, and Eve.Problems Christians have with Evolution: The Timetable

The first, and perhaps most obvious, problem most Christians have with the idea of evolution is the time-frame needed to fit any evolutionary model into a literal reading of Genesis 1. After all, if God created the cosmos including human beings, in 7, 24 hour days, then clearly there is no "time" for humans to evolve from anything. Instead, at one point in the past, humans did not exist. Then, at another point, humans did exist. Moreover, they existed fully formed and fully evolved. The point here is to say, the approach is concerned not so much with evolutionary theory itself as it is the time it took God to create humans. If God created humans in a few seconds on day 6 of the creation event, then any evolutionary theory is deemed immediately irrelevant.

However, as attested in the previous chapter, there are many sound Christian theories of the creation event that do not ascribe to a 7, 24 hour day, literalist theory of how God created the Cosmos. From Sacred week theories, to Gap theories, to Age-Day theories, to Revelation-Day theories, to Eden only theories (and more), each alternative approach adds significant possibilities to incorporate some form of evolutionary design into the equation if you want . By no means is this incorporation necessary, as scientists themselves seem to be changing their theories on evolution even as we speak. Because of this, it is important to remember that the goal is to simply appreciate and incorporate the best "truth" as we know it from both science and religious circles. If scientists change their theories of evolution (and they are definitely changing), then Christians ought to have the capacity to change what we think regarding those theories too. This is part of why it is important to not view the Bible as a science book, but also to not view scientific theory as immutable fact either. Certain truths are immutable. Others not so much. The key is to have flexibility where possible so we can incorporate the best of what both worlds have to offer as the human race grows in our depth of knowledge and understanding of whatever the issues may be.

Evolution that Eliminates God

The second problem many Christians have with evolution is that, in its purest form, evolution totally eliminates the role of God in the creation process. The idea is something akin to theorizing that the entire process of life development was unsupervised, not designed, random, chance, accidental, impersonal, with no purpose or plan, no intelligence behind any of it, and so forth. With this view, everything we see and know, every aspect of the cosmos from the smallest molecule to the greatest galaxies is nothing more than a cosmic accident. As for human beings, scientists point to some form of distinctly human existence emerging from the pre-human ancestors around 4 million years, and none of it includes the possibility of design. Instead it is accident, random chance, with no possibilities of a Creator or Intelligence behind it all.

At least one question Christian's ought to at least consider in this conversation though is simply this, "What does the presence of God anywhere in this evolution conversation have to do with a theory on how humans separated themselves from pre- human forms of 'ape-life' 4 million years ago?"And it is a fair question. It is one thing to talk about a theory of how humans evolved from primordial soup. It is quite another thing entirely to define any role that God might or might not play in such a process. It is one thing to say that the human race evolved from an ancestral couple that existed 4.4 million years ago. It is another thing entirely to include in those theories the idea that God had nothing to do with the design or creation of that ancestral couple.

Here is the point. Going back to the Galileo incident (and there are others), most logical people would agree that, in obvious cases where we are strictly talking science, the church needs to stay out of it. Why would this principle not also apply to the scientist who wants to discuss the role (or lack thereof) of God in a scientific process? If scientists want to tell us that evolution is the best possible explanation for human origins, then great. Give us the scientific theory. But then, move along. Beyond the scientific theory itself, it is no longer the job of the scientists to eliminate God from the conversation. Rather, it is the job of Christians to discern how to reconcile the "latest, greatest scientific theories" with the truths we hold dear in the church. And we can do that.

Even with evolution, if language is avoided that excludes any possibility for God to be involved in the process, then immediately a myriad of doors are opened as to the various ways God may or may not have been an integral part of the process. We will get to some of these possibilities in a moment.

Evolution Eliminates "Human" from Human Being

What makes a human, human? What does it mean to be distinctly human? What separates humans from animals, fish, birds? Is it our intelligence? After all, certain humans seem to exhibit very little intelligence, while certain animals such as whales and chimps seem to have high levels of intelligence. Is it our ability to communicate? If so, dogs bark, birds chirp, whales sing, and yet husbands and wives sometimes seem incapable of having even one single intelligent conversation. Good looks? How many birds, tigers, bears, elk are more attractive to you than some humans? Emotions? Let's be honest, how many of our pets have shown more (certainly more pleasant) emotions than many people you have known? Stopping here, it is easy to understand why some would conclude that there is no difference between many human beings and the animal kingdom. This then makes a decent argument for the elimination of God from the conversation. But it does lead to an important point. Is there a difference, and if so, what?

Ethics, Morals, and the Human Soul

Ethics - the ability to learn, choose, decide between right and wrong. Morals - the idea that there is a right and wrong. The human soul - that piece of unique, authentic, and distinctly human existence that allows us to love or to hate. Jesus had many sayings on these issues, such as, "Even if you gain the entire world, [become the next Bill Gates or Warren Buffet], but you become miserable along the way and lose your own soul, what good would that be for you? (Matthew 16:26)" Or, "Yes, there are people out there who can threaten you, even kill you, but don't worry about them, because the truth is, they can do nothing to harm your soul (Matthew 10:28)." Here's the point: Jesus said there is a soul. A soul. In so many respects, it is the soul that makes the primary, perhaps even only, difference between human beings and everything else in all the creation. Which matters ... why?

When it all comes out of the wash, we human beings really can very, very much act, behave, perhaps even be just like all the other animals. At times, no question, certain animals act much more "human" than we humans can act. After all, they don't call it the "rat race" for nothing. Ever felt like a caged animal? Ever felt like your dog or cat was a better excuse for a human being than one of your family members? If so, you are not alone. We all feel that way at times. Even more, the worst of human beings among us must be treated as caged animals, because outside of that, they are simply incompatible with anything we might consider a "normal human being." The reason I bring this up is because, regardless of whether a human suppresses, abuses, or even denies it, the soul is ultimately what separates human beings from the rest of life. And this of course, is where the rubber hits the road in our conversation about evolution and Christianity.

Who are the best of humans among us? What makes for our greatest examples of the human race? Is it those among us who have the most money, hoard the most money, and die rich? Is it those who have the most power, regardless of how they use it? Is it those who are having the most fun, and thus we simply envy their hedonism? Or, are the greatest humans among us people like Jesus Christ, Ghandi, Mother Teresa, Martin Luther King, Jr? If so, what makes them great? What makes them so special? Why did they have such amazing impact on our world? And even more, can we not agree that "what makes them special" goes against everything we know about the fundamental moral forces behind evolution and "survival of the fittest?"

What are the moral forces behind evolution? And the answer is, there are none. What are the imperatives that drive "survival of the fittest?" And the answer is, survival. Which implies what? Survival simply implies the person "doing the surviving" is going to do whatever it takes to survive. There are several very popular television shows based on this premise of survival. From Survivor, to Amazing Race, to Cutthroat Kitchen, the plot lines for each of these shows is simple: Pit the morality of the individual (or teams) against their inner moral compass. We all want to know, "when will their desire to 'win' trump their desire to be 'moral.'" Yes? Taken to its extreme, this desire for survival would mean that the "winner" would be the person or persons who are simply able to "win" the game regardless of how they go about it. Need to kill the elderly or handicapped to survive? Do it. Have someone slowing up the march towards the Promised Land? Leave them behind, and let them die. Someone on the hill that is impeding your path to the top? Knock them off. And countless people have lived just that very way. Consider Stalin. Consider Hitler. But are those people our heroes? In terms of survival of the fittest, they should be! And yet, for most people like that- people who have and hoard and crush and hurt- they are fiends not friends.

If we are honest with ourselves, there is no denying that something is going on here that completely undermines the entire argument of human beings evolving from a primordial slime with absolutely zero moral compass, much less soul, with survival of the fittest as our driving purpose. There is something going on, and it very much goes against, if not bemoans the very idea of survival of the fittest when it comes to human essence. For lions, bears, fish, birds, we accept survival of the fittest as a necessary and understandable fact of life. For humans to take such an approach is virtually unthinkable. Those who accept that are both in-human-e and a menace to society. On the other hand, those who embrace a deeper, ethical, moral standard, which is completely unexplainable through atheistic evolution, those who love the unlovable and care for the broken, these are the very ones who not only model the best of what humanity can be, in fact, they are modeling what makes humans "human" in the first place. How interesting that it is these very principles that Jesus says God is all about. For thinking people, these conclusions simply demand some type of common ground between the idea of a soul and God (the cause of morality) and the theories proposed by leading scientists on the origins of the human species.

Common Ground

Can science and religion (especially Christians) be friends concerning human origins? And the answer is, unequivocally, yes. However, per usual with all of these issues, there is no black and white answer to the questions at hand. Also per usual, a healthy balance must be found between what we hold true in our hearts or have learned in our past versus the new sources of information we learn from others, especially experts, that may challenge our assumptions and current ways of thinking. Given that, below are just a few common domain options to get the conversation jump-started (again, Wikipedia is an easy place to start). Note that there are a myriad of options both within and outside of what is presented here that, again, are both reasonable and defensible. It is not only acceptable, but desired that you will think this through, study your desired approach to its end, then come to your own conclusions. As we do this (become open-minded), not only are we liberated from the bondage of closed-minded thinking, but we find that such liberation to think and consider new possibilities for truth become absolutely transformative.

As for options, first, we consider Intelligent Design theory. There are several items to consider here. The fun part though is that, especially as a Christian, we are allowed to begin with what scientists say are their foundational tenets of evolutionary theory.

For example, you would embrace the idea that not only the cosmos, but life evolves. And life not only evolves, it adapts, has variation, and natural selection to a point, as well as various other ideas like mutation, even survival of the fittest, to a point. We learn the arguments, and we appreciate what the best scientists of our age teach us. But, then we add another piece.

The other critical piece is that we also embrace the idea that, whatever the scientific theory, the fingerprint of an Intelligent Designer exists behind every facet of cosmic organization. After all, what in all the universe organizes itself? Do computers organize themselves from nothing? Do brownies organize themselves from nothing? Cars, houses, boats, does anything self-organize? The answer is no. Computers have a programmer. Buildings have architects and builders. Cars have manufacturers. Cakes have the chef. And this isn't even remotely addressing issues of where the parts for the organization or organism come from to begin with. That is for another argument. What is for our purposes here is simply this: Even with all the parts in place, a car will never assemble or organize itself. It just doesn't happen. Complex, even simple, things require an Intelligent Designer, a Master Architect, a Programmer, an Organizer. To exclude such a Designer from the evolutionary process is to talk nonsense. To include such a Designer or Programmer in fact validates the idea that such an infinitely unlikely, if not impossible, process as evolution might in fact not only be possible, but perhaps even plausible.

An alternative view to which one might subscribe is the "Evolutionary Design" Theory. This theory sees evolution simply as a part of the process and progress of the Natural Laws that God Himself put into place. And for this one, again, we can appeal to science to teach us about evolution and even the Laws of Physics themselves. But when it comes to who made the Laws of Physics, science needs religion to fill in the blank. With this approach, one might believe that order, including the Laws of Physics, was created from chaos. One might believe that human life somehow evolved from that chaos too. But one can also believe that it was only from God that order created from chaos. God created, organized, set in motion, and sustains both the "materials" and the laws of physics that made the process possible that evolutionary theorists describe. In other words, God set all the parts of evolution in place; and, God continues to work both within and outside the scientific realm to see the entire process to its proper end.

Are there other possibilities? Of course. In fact, the range of possible solutions for the meeting place of science and religion concerning evolutionary theory is limitless. In fact, if humility is observed, the more you learn about both disciplines, the more options you will uncover. Ultimately, this leaves us created by God, but with a million possibilities as to how God did it. But that is the joy of the question. It is bigger than us, bigger than humanity, bigger than the greatest minds could put on paper. And shouldn't it be that way? After all, is it not both the cosmos and God we are talking about? If so, the lack of a perfect answer ought to in fact affirm both our science and our faith, not the opposite. Likewise, the more we learn about the wonders and complexity of our own existence, the greater appreciation we can have for both the God who created it all and the creation itself, including us.

Questions for Reflection:

1. Where do you think humans came from? Why?

2. Why do many Christians struggle with the idea of evolution?

3. What separates humanity from the animals?

4. Why are people who live by "survival of the fittest" fiends, not friends?

5. Why does the evolutionary argument of "survival of the fittest" actually detract from the validity of evolution itself?

6. How can a person believe in evolution and the Bible?

NOTES

CHAPTER 4

Science and The Future

I have always been a Star Trek fan. As far back as I can remember, if it wasn't the Voyager series, then it was The Next Generation. If not The Next Generation, then it was all the movies from First Contact to The Wrath of Khan. And if not the movies, it was the myriad of Star Trek television shows with the infamous, original Kirk, Spock, and McCoy. The appeal of these shows, for me at least, was the infinite possibilities offered by scientific advancements, discovery and exploration. After all, that is what makes the idea of space intriguing, yes? Incomprehensible size and scope, with incomprehensible resources that might provide limitless possibilities for the future. Star Trek makes the future seem amazingly bright, regardless of whether or not God is involved. After all, who needs God when we can look forward to "going where no one has gone before!" But therein lies the problem. What do scientists really tell us about the future of space and this place "where no one has gone before?" Do scientists themselves predict a Star Trek outcome? Or, are they anticipating a future that is far less encouraging? What do scientists say about the future, and how does that relate to our faith in God?

Entropyand the 2nd Law of Thermodynamics

If you want an almost incontrovertible proof of God's existence, look no further than energy. Energy? Yes, energy! Have you ever wondered where energy comes from? Have you ever wondered not simply how energy from the sun gets to the earth for us to process in solar panels, but rather where did the energy for the sun itself come from? We talked at length earlier about the Big Bang. Great. Bang. Big! An explosion of unimaginable proportions from a small speck of condensed matter (that came from nothing?) shoots cosmic matter to the far reaches of the universe. Yes. But, where did the energy from that explosion come from? And even more for our purposes, where is it going?

Scientists teach us a very common sense, but perhaps not intuitive, principle called entropy. Related to the 2nd Law of Thermodynamics, entropy basically says that all things, everything, are ultimately and methodically moving towards a state of rest. Just as cars need gas to run, just as food decays to dust, just as batteries deplete, just as humans will return to dust, so all things ultimately are moving towards a state of rest. And that really is all things. Not even the sun itself will last forever. Instead it is more like a candle that one day will simply burn out. Why does that matter?

The principle of entropy matters because it applies, not only to everyday life, but to the entirety of cosmic life. So, there was a Big Bang that started the cosmos off with great acclaim and fanfare. But then what? And it is the "then what" that is so very important for both scientists and Christians alike to understand. In so many respects, this is where the mechanism and the music of science and religion integrate and conjoin. In so very many respects, the portrait of our future provided by scientists provides yet another reason why science and religion need each other. Scientists have provided an excruciatingly clear picture of what the future holds, but often (certainly not always) it is not what we see from Hollywood or the press. In this, where science stops, religion picks up. And when we can incorporate both perspectives into our worldview, there is no question that the future becomes both more grounded and hope-filled for all Scientific Possibilities for our Future

What are scientists telling us about the future? You already know most of these arguments. One of the most obvious is the inevitable demise of a planet that has limited resources, because those resources are being depleted by a generally unconcerned populace. Of course, some people care. Unfortunately, it is not enough. And while it is not my purpose to argue the merits or not of environmental ethics, what is not up for debate is that something is going on that is negatively affecting our environment.

From polar caps, to melting glaciers, to rising sea levels, most of us are at least familiar with these environmental issues. Add to that, pollution, the depletion of wildlife, countless annihilation of various species of fish, the dying of ocean reefs, deforestation of rain forests, increasingly sparse fresh water resources, and on and on, the question is not, "what can we do to reclaim the greatness of our amazing planet earth?" Instead, the question now is, given the irreparable damage we have done and are currently doing, how long will our planet maintain human life given our current rate of resource depletion?

Then you have the Hollywood story. It is Bruce Willis flying the Space Shuttle into the jaws of an oncoming asteroid with a bevy of nuclear weapons to destroy the rock and save the world. Part of the appeal of such movies is that we know, if such an asteroid really were to hit, it would end all or at least a significant portion of life as we know it. Could this happen? Scientists tell us, absolutely. In fact, most believe it already has happened, so it is not a stretch to think it might happen again. The only difference being, Bruce Willis more than likely won't be there to save us.

Back to our entropy piece. How long will our resources last before this planet can no longer sustain life? Or the sun? How long is the sun going to last before this candle simply burns out? And when it does, what about human life then? But even more, how long will the cosmos last before it simply runs out of energy too? Often we don't pause to consider the ramifications, but if the Big Bang is true, then any "Bang" will eventually disperse into small sparks and a fizzle. Just like the huge fireworks at the July 4th displays, the initial "pop" is sounded, the point of light is seen rushing into the sky, the amazing, awe-inspiring "BOOM" of the firework at its peak explodes into an array of beautiful shapes and lights, but then what? It all ends with a fizzle. Inevitably, every "BANG" ends with a fizzle.

The story of our universe is very similar to the grandest firework on a July 4th spectacular. Scientists tell us it began with a bang, but will end with a fizzle. From the initial bang, everything we see and observe exploded from that initial point of matter. Since that time, everything we are able to see and observe has been moving at an unimaginable rate away from that initial exploding point. But here's the thing, scientists tell us there is no end to the expansion of the cosmos. There is no stopping point. There is no "we've made it, so now let's enjoy it" destination. What this means is, if ever we did actually invent the spaceship Enterprise and travel to the ends of the cosmos, what we would find is nothing. Why? It's because at the ends of the universe, all energy will have been completely used up and fizzled out. This means that nothing could remain there except a very cold, very dark, very barren wasteland. Why? Entropy. Why? As scientists explain, it is simply because, over time, all things move to a place of rest, not the opposite.

Stephen Weinburg, the 1979 Nobel prize winning physicist said it something like this. The more scientists unlock and discover all the intricacies and fascinations of the cosmos, unfortunately, the more it all seems pointless and futile. What a contrast to the message of Christianity that says, the more we understand it all, the more it leads to life.A Christian Alternative - The Promise of Religion

Part of my goal here is to continually revisit where we started. Part of the point is to at least open our eyes to the need of science for religion, and the need for religion to appreciate science. Both can lead us to God. Both can add to our appreciation and joy of life. If left alone, religion is myopic and incapable of appreciating the breathtaking intricacies of the God-given cosmos around us. Also if left alone, science is nothing more than depressing. Why? It's because there is so much good to be observed and enjoyed all throughout the cosmos, but without a "happy ending," then what's the use?

From the mountains, valleys, oceans and forests of our planet, to the stunning majesty of cosmic events like a supernova or black hole, all of it points to beauty that is both around and beyond us. Where science and religion ought to agree is that, from the molecular to the cosmic level, the creation is simply a wonder to behold. And most of us, scientists, Christian, and Christians who are scientists alike, really, really love what we see. Even more, we don't want to let it go. At issue then is the question, do we have to? And for this one, Christianity and the Bible really does offer an even more amazing story than what scientists tell us about the creation itself.

The Question is the Question

The very idea that we are even curious about life after death is an argument for something beyond life itself. Even more, the very idea that we dread death after life, is a further indicator that something else is going on here beyond what science can observe. At issue for us is the question, why do we dread death at all? And the answer is simple enough. We dread death because there are certain things in and about life that we simply have grown attached to, certain things we very much love and appreciate. We don't want to let them go.

Buddhists argue that suffering is caused by our clinging attachments to both life and the things (including people) in life that we have grown to love and appreciate. There is little doubt that, if we choose to un-attach ourselves from everything good and meaningful in life, then certainly very little suffering will ensue should we lose those things (including our own lives). But the thing is, even in Buddhism, the idea is that there is a natural tendency in all of us to in fact love, appreciate, attach ourselves to, and enjoy various parts of the creation. There is just an innate part of every human being that sees the world and the cosmos and falls in love with it. At the heart of the best science is a deep appreciation for the beauty of the creation in its various forms. Why do we all love the creation so? Why do we want to hold on to it? Why are we anxious, even afraid of letting it go? The Christian answer is that God intended it that way, that God wants us to love, appreciate, and enjoy the creation. After all, God Himself felt the same way. God created it all, and when he looked over what He had made, it was very good. God loved it too, and before we did.

The best scientific discoveries must have come with a great exclamation, "wow, that is awesome!" Or, "we did it!" Or, "can you believe that!" Or, perhaps, "that is very good!" It is the silence that fills a space when you observe something that defies description. It doesn't take much to imagine the excitement of the first person who ever observed the rings of Saturn through the first telescope. It doesn't take much to imagine the response of the first person to see pictures from the Hubble. Can you imagine how an astronaut feels the first time they are up in space looking back at the earth? Silent Awe. Amazement. And yes, it is very good. And we don't want to let that goodness go, especially once we discover how far-reaching and vast the goodness extends. It is powerful. It is transformative. Because of this, a part of every human being cringes at the thought of having to give up "the good" creation that is around us.

Well, Christianity says we don't have to give it up. In fact, the Bible is pretty clear that God never intended for either us or Him to give it up. Even more, the Bible also fills in the rest of the story that science simply cannot write. And it is such a beautiful story. In the beginning, God hovered over the vast expanse of nothingness, and then God said, light! And BANG, there was a cosmic explosion that literally illuminated the universe. From that starting point, with intelligence and amazing design, God guided that initial explosion into galaxies, solar systems, stars, and yes, even planet earth. On this earth, God then created water, dry land, trees, plants, fish, animals, birds and all that we know of life. But in the midst of that life, God created human beings. Human beings who were like God, made in God's image, with the ability to what? Love, yes. But for our purposes, with the ability to appreciate the good creation that God had made too.

It is important that we realize God wants us to appreciate His creation. It is also important that we realize we are the only species on the planet that will gaze into the stars in admiration and awe. It is important to realize that there is a huge difference between humanity and monkeys, because you will never find a monkey attempting to build a spacecraft, a telescope, or a skyscraper for no other reason than to explore "what is out there" because it is so beautiful and interesting. Part of the separation between humanity and all other life is our passion for discovery, our love of creating, our appreciation of the creation itself, and, note well, our worry that we will lose it in death. All of these are arguments for the existence of God, but that is not the point. The point is that we agree with the Bible that, when we look out over all that was made, it is good. Not perfect, no. It's almost as if parts of the creation are a bit flawed, polluted, and stained. But the goodness remains, and this is precisely what we love so much when we head out to the deer stand, the lake, the mountains, the beach, or when we look through various telescopic lenses from the micro to macroscopic.

Which matters ...why? This matters precisely because the Bible says God will not give up on His good creation, instead, one day God will redeem it. This matters precisely because God did not create all that we observe, give up on it and walk away. This matters precisely because, whenever we identify wonderfully good things in and around us, when we observe majestic pictures of a nebula in space down to the tiny frame of a newborn baby in its mother's arms, its end will not come with a fizzle in darkness. Instead, God's answer to it all is redemption. Redeem. To reclaim. To restore. To retrieve. To recover. To repossess. Yes, God has allowed us to be caretakers, stewards of the world around us. However, God has not given it to us. And one day, God will take back what God owns. And that is a good thing, because when God takes back, or redeems His creation, He will then restore it to its former glory (this is the 2nd heaven). The primary difference being, this time, we (those who truly love God and want to be in his family) will get to be a part of it, only without the problems, suffering, pollution, distortions or the pain.

What is that going to look like? And the truth is, nobody knows the full picture. It is just too great. But, what we do know is mind boggling.

How do we know that? Ironically enough, science has taught us. Talk about religion needing science, how ironic that when Christians talk about heaven, more often than not they are appealing to what scientists have taught us down here on earth. We appeal to space, the vastness of the cosmos, the discoveries of scientists from biologists to astrophysicists, to the oceans, mountains, and valleys that scientific discoveries have allowed us to explore. This is at least one foundational reason why scientific discoveries should not turn us away from God, rather they should lead us to God, because those very discoveries give us deepening insights into what God has in store for our redeemed future. This redeemed future necessarily includes the very best of what we discover today, only better. For scientists, how amazing that with every discovery of something good in our universe, they are but sniffing the appetizer of the main course to come. Talk about friends, science and Christianity are in fact family, if only we would open our eyes to see it.

Describing this juxtaposition of the natural world (revealed by science) and the redeemed creation to come (revealed by religion), CS Lewis offers this explanation through the lens of some children who had just entered the redeemed creation. He says it something like this (I have paraphrased a bit) in his book, *The Last Battle:*

It seemed to be early and the morning freshness was in the air. They kept stopping to look around and to look behind them, partly because it was so beautiful but partly because there was something about it which they couldn't understand. Where do you suppose this is? one of them asked. I don't know, said her friend, but it reminds me of a place I've been before. Only, the mountains, they look like the mountains I remember. Yet, they are so much bigger, so much more beautiful, so much more majestic. And there, those hills, the nice, rolling pleasant ones and the majestic ones behind, they remind me of a place in the south. But, they are different. They have so many more colors and they are so much prettier than I remember. It's like they are more like the real thing than before.

One of their friends, an eagle, spread his wings and soared 30 or 40 feet up into the air, circled around and then came back down to alight on the ground. Everyone, he said. Listen. We have all been blind. We are only beginning to see where we are. From up there I have seen it all. The great rivers, the beautiful mountains. It's all here as it used to be, it has not been destroyed. Only, it has been transformed, re-created, redeemed. It's as if, what we remember from the old world was a copy, a shadow of the real world, which is here. (*The Last Battle*, by CS Lewis, MacMillan Publishing, 1956, p. 159-162).

Questions for Reflection:

1. What is entropy?

2. How does entropy relate to how scientists explain the end of the universe?

3. How does the idea of Christian redemption change the picture of endings for our cosmos?

4. What do you think the cosmos and our earth looked like in the very beginning, when it was very good?

5. What of the original "good Creation" is still available for us (humanity) to observe and enjoy today?

6. What do you think the cosmos and our earth will look like when it is redeemed? (What will be refined away? What will remain?)

NOTES

CHAPTER 5

God and The Big Bang

So where do you stop? Should we talk about aliens? After all, there is a great deal of interest concerning science and the potential of alien life. Is it possible to believe in aliens and Christianity? Sure. Or, what about God and medicine? Should our perspective on the medical sciences affect how we believe God works in our world? Of course. Or, physics. Shouldn't the existence of the Laws of Physics and where those laws came from warrant at least a conversation between scientists and Christians? Or other debates, such as those involving the church and Copernicus, or the church and Darwin. Or other themes, such as models of interaction, verification, falsification, theoretical anomalies, evolutionary psychology, quantum mechanics, and on and on the list goes. What is the answer to all these questions between religion and science? The answer? Well, again, what do you think?

If nothing else, the point here is to say, we should think, and it's OK to come to our own conclusions regarding these issues. After all, not one of these science and religion issues relates to salvation. As such, have faith, but also seek understanding. On the other hand, much can be said for seeking understanding so that you can have faith. And that's the joy of particularly the Christian faith, because the more answers you seek, the more answers you will find. It is simply amazing how, when we will open ourselves to new possibilities and new answers, the Gospel of Jesus Christ just makes more and more sense. And that includes answers provided by most scientists. In so, so many respects, science and religion support each other. They are not mutually exclusive, rather, in far more ways than one, they are in fact mutually inclusive. Why? Because both fields seek, discover, and share truth and knowledge. Both fields seek, discover, and share perspectives on our world and beyond that are both necessary and helpful for a holistic understand of life and the place of humanity in the cosmos. For far too long, people have claimed that, to be a Christian, you have to maintain a blind ignorance to the obvious truths science teaches us about the world around us. For far too long, others have claimed that, to be a scientist, you cannot also recognize the creator God who so obviously had a major role to play in the formation and continuance of the world around us. But the "real truth" is, both are right, and both fields need each other to be complete.

Religion Needs Science

Both fields need each other. I could say it a million times and feel the statement is not being heard, but it's true. Science needs religion, and religion needs science. Let's add a few more points on the latter, then we will wrap this up with the former. Do you know why religion needs science too?

Just 600 years ago, the Western world was mired in the Dark Ages. The Dark Ages were called "dark" precisely why? Well, for one, because the entire populace was convinced of "realities" that were false. The world was flat. "Bleeding" people led to healing. Plagues were caused by witchcraft. When it rained, God was crying. When a hurricane hit, it was God's wrath. Seriously?

Enter science. Enter human curiosity to explain and cure diseases, not with bleeding, but with penicillin. Christian or not, tell me we aren't better offer understanding that God doesn't kill people, rather Ebola, heart attacks, viruses, malaria, cancer, whatever are the causes of death. Again, it is not superstition or some warped understanding of God, rather the cause of so many of our problems is perfectly explainable. Does "religion" really benefit when we believe God controls all things, including disease and malnutrition? Does "religion" really benefit when we believe that God controls all things like earthquakes and tornadoes? That God controls all things like giving children birth defects, even though the parents were alcoholics? It is one thing to offer a qualified "God is in Control," but it is another thing entirely to actually believe such a statement as if we are still living in the 1300s.

It is one thing to say that God can work good out of bad situations, but it is something else entirely to say God causes disease, suffering, plaques, earthquakes, famine and pestilence. Make no mistake, religion needs science. Christianity needs scientists to explain why so many of these bad things happen, and even more how the world simply works. And, quite literally we all should thank God for the scientists who led us out of the Dark Ages into a more balanced, holistic approach to faith today. Science has fundamentally taught us that God is not in the virus directing it to make you ill, or in your heart causing it to fail, or in your steering wheel causing it to crash if you get drunk. These things are simply the result of Natural Law, the Laws of Physics, of science. Yes, God gave us the Laws of Physics and Natural Law, but God also gave us brains to learn those laws so that we could better understand how He does and does not work in the world.

Additionally, religion needs science, because it is precisely through science that we begin to glimpse the true nature, majesty, and authority of the God we claim to worship. What does this look like? Well, because of science, now we know God is not stuck on some flat earth, between 2 layers of water, with sea monsters on one side and a great abyss on the other. No. Instead, because of Space Shuttles, Hubble telescopes, and microwave radiation studies, we now know that God created a universe of billions upon billions of galaxies. And in those billions upon billions of galaxies, there are trillions of stars and anomalies and gaseous formations, all of which stagger the mind.

And what sounds more like an omnipotent God, to create the entire universe in 7 little days, or to do it in a process of almost 14 billion years, a number that defies comprehension when you try to put it to paper? What sounds more like God, to put a few points of light in the sky we call "The Bear," or to view those lights through the Hubble telescope to reveal not just a few points of light, but an infinite array of stars so vast that the human mind cannot even comprehend what we can see from the Hubble, much less what is really out there. Seriously, are the scientists pointing us away from or towards the existence of God? And my answer, hands down, is toward Him. Make no mistake on this one, at least one primary reason people in religion need to listen to scientists is because scientists remove superstition from our faith and they expand our minds as to the incomprehensible majesty and nature of God's being.

Science Needs Religion Too

But it goes both ways, because for every positive development in science, you have someone, somewhere who will find a way to use that development negatively. And this really gets to the heart of the matter. When it all comes out of the wash, what is the single greatest problem facing humanity today? Is it, the right technology simply has not been invented yet? Or is it something far more personal than that? Let's work this through for a moment.

Is our greatest problem the fact that people get cancer, leukemia, or Alzheimer's, and medical scientists have not fond a cure? Is our greatest problem the fact that we haven't discovered a renewable energy source like cold fusion? Is our greatest problem that we haven't developed the technology to drive a car that gets 500 miles to the gallon and emits no pollution?Is our greatest problem environmental erosion or Global warming? Is our greatest problem world hunger or Ebola? What is the greatest problem facing the human race today?

Scientists tell us that humans have been evolving over something like the past 4.4 million years. Awesome. In any period throughout that course of time, do any of us believe human beings have become any nicer, more loving, less greedy, more compassionate? We know the answer. It is an authoritative "no." Across the globe, we are still murdering, raping, stealing, cheating, lying, abusing, and on and on. And not just to one another, we are doing it to our earth as well. We know the rain forests can never be replaced, and yet we cut them down anyway. We know countless species of fish can never be replaced, and yet we fish them to extinction anyway. We know, we are aware, we see it, and yet we don't care. Genocide? It is still happening. In 2014, there have been beheadings in our world. Seriously? Prostitution? Still exists. Slavery? Yep. Child pornography. Still here. Need I go on? What is the greatest problem facing humanity today? We all know the answer. Science can never fix it. In fact, in so many ways, science is making it worse.

It just needs to be said, because often the scientists among us conveniently neglect to consider the implications from these questions. But consider, what is the cause of the bulk of so many greenhouse emissions that scientists themselves are saying are killing our planet, depleting the Ozone layer, and giving so many of our children asthma? Is it not technology invented by the scientists? What was the bedrock foundation behind the industrial revolution that has created a world monster with an insatiable appetite for natural resources that will never be sated, even if it kills the very world it is eating? The answer is science. And if we really want to get personal, what is the one group of people in all the history of the world that created the weapons capable of annihilating all life on that very world? The answer, again, science. Scientists invented the nuclear bomb. The examples are limitless. Go back to Sept 11, 2001, and describe what you see in New York. You put even the most mundane of scientific advancements into the wrong hands, and what do you have? And, literally, God help us all if nuclear weapons ever get into the wrong hands. When it is all said and done, science and newer technology can never save us from the real problems faced by the human race. For that, something very very different is required. Which brings us to Jesus Christ.

A Christian ParadigmSo what's the answer? Is there an answer?

Simply put, yes. Yes, there is an answer. And of all people, the answer comes from the One who started it all. How ironic that God, the God who created it all from the Big Bang, who intelligently designed it all, who put the entire package together, that God would come into our world and give us the answer to the real problem faced by his children, humanity. And here is the answer God gave to our problems. When God visited us humans in the person of Jesus Christ, here is the solution He offered: unconditional love. Sound trite? Cliché? Well, maybe. But answer me this, what is the solution to the problem of potential nuclear warfare? What is the answer to the problem of greed, slavery, cheating, lying, stealing? Even environmental problems, think on this and it is hard to deny. Love could solve the world's environmental crisis, if people would authentically and genuinely love each other, care for the needs of all others, and yes, if they would truly love the planet too. You care for those you love. You do not abuse, rape, and pillage those you love. You do spend your money, not on warfare, but on food, clothing, medicine, shelter to give to those you love. And "those" in this instance includes people, our planet, everything. Love is a game-changer. What would the creation really be like, if everyone truly and genuinely loved everyone else, treated everyone else with love and respect, treated the planet with love and respect, and made it their life's goal to give more than they receive? Yet, this is exactly what God, the creator, said we should do, and this concerns both how we use the planet (ie, through scientific advancements) and how we relate to it and each other as well.

Conclusion

So here it all is in a nutshell. Imagine a world, where religion fundamentally appreciates, celebrates, and applauds science for all the ways in which that science opens our eyes from ignorance and superstition. Imagine a world where religion appreciates how science has taught us of the vast and infinite possibilities regarding the God-created cosmos all around us. In this, imagine a world where religion tries really hard, not to involve itself in scientific matters that do not concern religion. At the same time, imagine a world where science discovers and appreciates all the intricacies of the cosmos, but it is governed by the ethic of love and concern for both the earth and all people. Imagine a science that is open to embracing the idea of God and the solutions of God as to what truly ails our planet and our people. If that were to actually happen, in truth, would it not be one of the best solutions imaginable? And even more, my premise is that it is! Both science and religion are given to us by God. As such, both are right, and our world is fundamentally flawed without the best of what both have to offer. It is only when we learn to appreciate and integrate both fields of truth into our perspectives that we ourselves will become intellectually liberated and spiritually whole. Science needs religion. Religion needs science. Get this right, and everyone wins.

Questions for Reflection:

1. Why does religion need science?

2. Why does science need religion?

3. How has the antagonism between science and religion jaded current (postmodern) generations against both fields of truth?

4. How might we (humanity) begin the healing process to allow science and religion to be both friends and partners in moving humanity towards a better (more holistic) future?

NOTES

What's Next?

<u>Christian Logic</u>
<u>3</u>

*Look for Christian Logic 1, 2 & 3 on Audible/Ebook

*Check out FB

Dr.   Thomas   Childs

ABOUT THE AUTHOR

Dr. Thomas Childs grew up in Fairhope, Alabama, attending Baldwin county schools before graduating from Fairhope High School. He earned a B.M. degree in Jazz Studies (magna cum laude) from Loyola University, New Orleans, a Master of Divinity Degree (with biblical languages) from Southwestern Baptist Theological Seminary in Fort Worth, TX, studied at the Goethe Institute in Manheim Germany for a Summer, a Master of Theological Studies (cum laude) from Perkins School of Theology at Southern Methodist University, and his Doctorate of Ministry Degree (with honors) from St Paul School of Theology in Kansas City, Missouri.

Thomas has toured with the Christian band TRUTH, as well as playing in the New Orleans Symphony, the New Orleans Saints Jazz Band, the Desire Brothers band, the Harmon Lights jazz band, and others. Additionally, Thomas was the first chair trumpet player in the state of Alabama All-State competition, first chair in the Southern United States Honor Band,

and the Outstanding Music Major for Loyola Univ in 1993.

Thomas' church resume includes being the founding pastor of the LifePoint United Methodist Church, as well as being the pastor of the Dido United Methodist Church, the Blooming Grove United Methodist Church, and the Dresden United Methodist Church.

Thomas received the 2000 Morris Walker Clergy award for the Central Texas Conference of the United Methodist Church. Thomas has been an adjunct faculty for teaching Christian Leadership in the clinical pastoral education program at Harris Methodist Hospital, as well as teaching Christian Leadership at Texas Wesleyan University.

Thomas also has served as the Director of the St Andrews UMC building project in the Waxahachie District of the Central TX Conference in 1998- 1999, as well as serving as the Host Operations Director for the 2008 General Conference of the United Methodist Church in Fort Worth, TX from 2004-2008.

Thomas is married to Dr. Gladys Childs and they have one child, Scott.

Made in the USA
Middletown, DE
06 June 2023